The Wisdom Found in Words

Jerry Hlava

PublishAmerica
Baltimore

First printing

ISBN: 1-4137-2731-X
PUBLISHED BY PUBLISHAMERICA, LLLP
www.publishamerica.com
Baltimore

Printed in the United States of America

Foreword

Before you read on in this book, I would like to share something with you. The words and proverbs found in this book came from my father. He has shared them with my brothers and me over the years, and now he shares them with his grandchildren. Some of these words he has carried with him through his life, passed on to him from his parents and grandparents in the Czech Republic. Some of these words he has put together as examples of what he has learned throughout his life, not only as in immigrant, but also as a successful businessman, loving father, and devoted grandfather.

We have encouraged him to put these into a book form so that others can learn from him, just as we have. Some of what you will find in this book is ages old, and some of these you may have already heard. Take a few moments with each one. You will certainly gain some insight into life, family, society, and yourself.

The illustration for the cover art of this book was created from the inspiration that these words have given me over the years. I feel that it captures a sense, or a feeling that these words provide. The art expresses a flow of feeling and thought that one has when learning something new. This

image will change each time you see it. It will teach you something new, just as the wisdom found in the words within this book. The interpretation of this image will have different meaning to you at different stages in your life, just as the wisdom found in the words within this book. The image and the words are, in a sense, a union of line and poetry, imagination and insight. Refer to them both throughout your life, and you will be certain to find richness in your soul.

All this being said, it is my great pleasure to introduce you to my father and his words of wisdom. Jerry Hlava, the wisest man I have ever known.

- Patty Hlava

Preface

Words of wisdom were verbally passed down for centuries from one generation to another, from family to family, to show the people theirs shortcomings and to prevent them from getting hurt on their way through life. The wisdom found in these words will help you to see the people around you. Not as they appear, but as whom they are. The wisdom found in these words will prevent you from fighting in life at those times when you can only lose for another one's gain. The wisdom found in these words comes only from parents and grandparents with common sense, knowledge, and experience. The wisdom found in these words grows with observation, knowledge, and time.

Don't be surprised if you do not understand all of them at first, rest assured, you will in time. For example:

"Seed the wind and you will harvest a hurricane. "

In this book you will find over 600 words of wisdom that nobody will teach you and very few know. They are here for you, to help you on your way through life. They will help you to think through things and to see more clearly so you that you can live in harmony with others. Also to prevent you from making many mistakes in life. It is up to you if you

want to use them. These words are as important in your life as reading and math. Refer to them in your times of trouble and they will provide you with the strength you seek.

It is my honor to present you, as I have shared with my family, the Words of Wisdom.

Your father, grandfather and friend,

Jerry Hlava

The Wisdom Found in Words

You cannot break a brick wall with your head.

A smart man does not fight. A smart man uses his brain, not his fists.

Lies have short legs with which to run.

You and you alone have the power to shape your destiny.

Truth will always win in time.

Where the devil cannot go, he will send a woman in his place.

You decide and God will change.

Mature mills grind slow, but sure.

How you make your bed is how restful you will sleep.

Luck will very rarely walk with an idiot.

Learn and you'll have a good life.

If you want to learn, you must make some sacrifices.

What you play with, that is what you end up with.

Honor your parents and you will have good life on this earth.

Don't ever think that you are the only "smart one."

With a smile on your face and a hat in your hand, you can walk through the world penniless.

Don't be ashamed to bow, gold is always found at your feet.

With envy, jealousy, pride and arrogance you'll never get too far.

There are things between Heaven and Earth that you will never understand.

If you get up early you will get further in the day.

Nothing is ever as you see it.

All people wear seven masks. In your lifetime, you will never remove the last one.

You can trust, but you must check.

Lies repeated a hundred times become the truth to ninety-five percent of the population.

Naked you came, and naked you will leave.

If you are born under a bench then there you will stay there all of your life.

A good suit is the thing that separates man from animal.

If you don't understand something give it to a horse, he has a bigger head.

If you choose to live with the wolves, you must howl with them as well.

Always sing the song of the person whose bread you are eating.

If you want to catch a bird you must sing a nice song.

Birds with the same feathers will always fly together.

Animals don't kill for pleasure.

Animals keep their genes pure.

Nature gives and nature takes.

Not all of the clouds that you see will produce rain.

You never can walk in the same forest twice and you cannot step in the same river twice.

Calm water in time undermines the banks.

Only time can tell.

You will never know your time and your hour.

You can't accomplish a task without knowledge and vision.

You can accomplish anything if you set your mind to it.

Two off your best friends: persistence and determination.

Your spirit will guide you to your destiny.

After the storm there is always silence.

Water and fire are good servants but danger is their master.

You must crawl first before you can walk.

Without your brain, you can feed only one mouth.

Befriend the child in your heart and feed his dreams. They will give
you strength when you need it most.

To be on time is the honor of the Kings.

Don't judge a book by its cover.

Tell me what you read and I will tell you who you are.

Knowledge separates man from animal.

How many languages you know is how many times you are a
human being.

By the clothes a man wears, you can judge what kind of man he is.

You can't deceive or lie to your parents with out their knowing.

You learn by mistakes.

Life is easy if you listen.

As a child, you often play with what your heart desires. Use this as a
stool to enhance your adulthood.

Silence is worth gold, talking is worth silver.

Your best friends in conversation are, who, where, how, why and when.

Don't speak if you're not asked.

Believe in yourself.

Don't trust anybody's promises, only their deeds.

Don't ever trust smooth talkers.

As you judge yourself, that is how others judge you.

You can't stop hunger in the desert with a golden plate.

An empty drum always makes a lot of noise.

Don't ever look for a reward before you finish the work.

Wisdom comes with age.

Everybody has only one true friend in his or her lifetime.

Two is advice, three is always betrayal.

Don't ever follow a crowd with banners.

A pie in the sky cannot fill your stomach.

A man with a full stomach cannot understand a hungry man.

If you wish to understand the person's troubles, you must walk in his shoes.

Nothing is forever.

Your life is what you make of it.

What the eyes don't see doesn't hurt the heart.

Don't ever believe everything you hear.

A government who oppresses his people always has a strong army at hand.

Don't ever believe everything you read in the daily paper, the paper can take everything.

Your parents and your environment shape your path in life.

Healthy body - healthy soul.

* You are the master of your destiny.

You will know the culture of a people by their toilets.

Healthy family is the base for healthy nation.

A wounded animal is dangerous, so is a wounded man.

Don't ever become an informer; the price is too high.

Don't ever betray anybody for money. You will lose your honor and friends, sometimes even your life.

Brainless people always do dirty work.

Nothing is far from the truth.

Betrayal brings misery to all involved.

Man brings misfortune always upon himself by himself.

* You will never learn enough, no matter how long you live.

Knowledge is the mother of success.

You can be born only once, and only to one mother.

Don't believe in the fatherland, all the Earth is yours to live in.

You don't want ever want to know how hotdogs or laws are made.

Rules can be bent.

Laws are passed to control the masses.

You will find out who your friends are only in the critical times.

Your belief will make your body healthy.

Not even a chicken scratches around for free.

You always get what you deserve.

Grass on other side of the fence always looks greener.

If you a dig hole for somebody be careful so you that don't fall into it yourself.

Give and somebody else will give you, wish good and somebody else will wish good for you also.

Don't play with the fire.

Don't make waves.

Be careful what you wish for.

It is more than likely that you will become the same as the people you associate with.

The eyes are the windows to the soul.

True beauty lies beneath the surface.

Truth cannot be always told.

Truth in words always hurts.

Don't get possessed with revenge.

If you don't work you cannot eat.

Stay with the profession you know best.

A gift that is given twice brings good luck.

If you wish to beat a dog, you will find the stick.

Wood always will be wood and an idiot will be always an idiot.

You can't teach old horses new tricks.

You can bring horses to the water, but you cannot make them drink.

Pigs will be always pigs.

Only a baby has an honest smile.

Many people will jump into the fire for a dollar.

Don't try to put out a fire if it does not threaten you.

Don't take your words lightly.

Cruel words cause ever-lasting pain.

You can make a fool of man sometimes, but you cannot fool everybody all the time and every time.

If the shoe fits, wear it.

A smart person doesn't question things, and stupid people don't know any better.

Long hair equals small brain.

You never argue with an idiot or a drunk.

What you don't want then lend it to somebody.

Never lend money to relatives.

Small shit smells the most.

Devil and politicians try to steal your soul.

If you wish to leave something behind you on this Earth have a son, seed trees, and write a book.

What you don't want somebody to do to you, don't do that to them.

You have to wait for your time to come, just as a goose has to wait for the grass to grow.

How you eat by the table is how you treat the people around you.

Even pigs know when they have had enough.

If you don't like yourself, you cannot like anybody else.

Don't start what you can't finish.

Your personality is revealed by how you slice your bread.

If you don't respect books then you don't respect others.

The wolf and the rabbit cannot live together.

Cold hand equals cold heart.

Stripes and promotions were designed to exploit men.

Scare tactics keep the herd together.

A man with a gun can keep people by the wall, but not for long.

Animals are hunted once a year; man is hunted once in a lifetime.

If you don't find money on a happy man then you will for sure find money on the man who cries all the time.

If you cannot fight them then join them and they will fall from within.

One rotten apple spoils the whole basket.

A system of two parties always oppresses people.

Eye for an eye and a tooth for a tooth.

Only a woman can hold family a together.

Woman is the neck and the man is the head.

A tree is the best listener.

Even Mother Nature shakes her fleece.

It is a woman that makes a man successful.

A dog is man's best friend.

Salt is worth more than gold.

Rough bag, rough patch.

Pain is but one step in the process of healing.

A stupid and ambitious man can destroy a nation.

No brain - no gain.

Deceivers always come with flashing banners.

Food is the most effective weapon.

A squeaky wheel gets the most grease, but sometimes it gets replaced.

A man is like dough in a woman's hand, he can be molded into any shape.

The rooster always dominates farm.

You cannot have two roosters on the same pile.

God gave you two hands to feed one mouth.

Don't ever buy a rabbit in bag.

A goat is the best gardener.

Thieves and stupid men are the best policeman.

Every doctor should have his own cemetery.

In desperation everybody calls on his or her mother and God.

Divide and you can rule.

The victor writes history: ten percent fat and thirty percent lean.

Ninety-five percent of people don't think, three percent of the people think they think, two percent of the people think.

Idiots and followers are the most dangerous people.

Only cows follow the bull over the cliff.

A coin always has two sides.

Let me print money and I don't care who is the King.

Money does funny things to people.

Don't ever look for money, look for deeds and the money will come.

Most people appreciate their parents after they are gone.

You always wonder why you didn't learn more.

Profession has a golden bottom.

Patience brings roses.

With only honesty you will not get too far.

A good person always finishes last.

If you don't do it, then somebody else will.

Everybody is replaceable.

Work while the steel is hot.

You can't get anywhere with a lazy mouth.

If luck gets tired, he will sometimes, he will sit even for an idiot.

What kind of store - that kind of keeper.

The smart one always looks for equal partner.

A man who blames somebody else is the one who is responsible.

Man who sees has twice as much.

Don't ever judge the presents you get, all presents are given from the heart.

Always respect an older person, one day you will be there too.

Listen once; hear twice.

Think twice before you talk.

God will help you if you help yourself.

Nothing is for free.

Honest people are hard to find.

Don't live without a goal.

Aiming high brings happiness in time.

Even a bum on the street has something to teach you.

Don't travel through your life alone.

Stand your ground. Don't let anybody control your destiny.

What you can see in your mind is obtainable.

What you cannot see, you cannot get.

Live up to your means, not beyond them.

Don't take advice from the man who has worked for you a long time.

You cannot get up without taking the steps one at a time.

Share your food, but never your thoughts.

Your secret in somebody else's head is not a secret anymore.

If you want somebody to know your secret write it down and leave it on the table.

A man who is drowning will try to hold onto even a straw.

Every living thing has a purpose in its life.

You have no control over events.

Even smart people get burned.

If you're looking for it, you will find it.

Sit in the corner and maybe somebody will find you.

If you want something badly enough you will get it.

If I have friends like you I don't need an enemy.

A new broom sweeps well.

As you see yourself that's how you see others.

Nobody knows you better than you know yourself.

Fish and visitors smell in three days.

Life is too short to worry.

Don't ever be scared of your enemy or others, pay attention to their numbers, they must sleep and eat.

An expert is usually from a hundred miles away.

Apples never fall far away from the trees.

Blood is thicker than water.

TV is the cheapest babysitter.

Taxes are robbery under the gun.

The names of servants to the ruling class are on every corner. The names of idiots are on every pole.

It is always dark under a lamp.

You can't outrun time.

Good advice is worth more than gold.

A credit card is a passport to slavery.

Friendship and business do not mix.

All nations and corporations have only one leader and he always is faceless and nameless to the people.

If you decide where you want to go, you will always find people on the way to help you.

How you call in the woods that is how you get your message back.

In death everybody is equal.

Spirit never dies.

A bird in the hand is better than a pigeon on the rooftop.

Where sun doesn't visit, the doctor will.

One apple a day keeps doctor away.

Measure twice, cut once.

Misplaced love brings misery and sometimes death.

Eat breakfast by yourself, share lunch with friend and dinner give to your enemy.

Don't walk into a bar without money.

Love can move mountains.

Time is forever.

Love brings happiness.

Even the hardest rock will die in time.

No doctor can help you if you don't help yourself.

You kiss the shoes that kick you and you bite the hand that feeds you.

All beautiful things have thorns.

Beauty loses its appeal in time.

Don't get attached to material things.

Enjoy life like a bird, but not as a pigeon.

Nobody can walk through life without scratches.

The sun does not shine every day.

You cannot make time go by faster.

As day and night is happiness and sadness.

Keep your friends close, and your enemies closer.

There is power and security in masses.

Every living thing knows they must save for bad times.

You cannot go to heaven or hell before your time.

Love must be nourished.

A drop every day is better than rain.

Love is the most beautiful thing. It gets better with the time and lasts forever.

You cannot take all your possessions to the grave.

What you learn in early age is what you will find in old age.

Only fools think they know everything.

A man who creates, doesn't destroy.

Animals fight for survival – man fights for greed.

Alcohol, envy, ambition, greed and jealousy can destroy a man.

Don't ever burn bridges behind you. You will need them on your way back.

Don't ever destroy the steps up. You never know how soon you'll need them on way down.

Cleaning less is half of your health.

In good times, time goes by fast, in bad times it goes by slowly.

Inherited wealth loses its value and is wasted in no time.

A small fish is safer.

Bad memories and bad experiences hold many people back from achieving their goals.

Everything looks beautiful from distance.

The most unappreciated profession is the farmer, but without him and his knowledge we all will starve.

The bad times will teach you a new profession if you want to survive.

Trees reach maturity in five years, dogs in two years and the man sometimes past his forties.

Everyone gives some time, but not to everybody.

Peace on earth will be achieved after all nations are shaken of all bloodsucking fleeces.

Many people strive in life to be famous, rich, and powerful but only a few achieve this and many of them for only a short period of time.

Many people strive to spend their resources to acquire knowledge, but only a handful succeeds in life.

Very few people strive for love, family, and happiness. Only a few have these precious things in life.

A soldier's profession is full of people looking for adventure and running away from social problems.

Life on the Earth is a living hell for many people.

Taste of heaven on the Earth is short-lived.

Man's will is stronger than anything else you know.

Life is a whip and we are her children.

Every nation deserves the leader they have.

All the answers lie in nature.

If you understand nature your life is easy and full of surprises.

God is full of promises and Devil is full of deeds.

You'll never know if you can swim until you try.

Speak from your heart and you will always speak the truth.

It is not luck, but determination and persistence that get you the things you have.

You cannot live by bread alone.

If you want to achieve and fulfill your dreams you must sacrifice and never give up.

A smile is the best defense – playing dumb is the second best defense.

Do not fight if you cannot win.

A woman is the pillar of a nation.

Not every tree can assure the life of its offspring to maturity.

Colors are the pride of the owner.

Some people try to show off with somebody else's feathers.

What is yours, is mine. What is mine is none of your business.

You cannot swim against the current.

Do not wish to fly, wish to soar.

Not every mirror reflects a true image.

Life is a big theater and you never know what will appear on the next stage.

Forbidden fruit tastes the best.

Sometimes even the heavens cry.

In marriage the love goes through the stomach.

Many let others drill their knees for a penny.

If somebody offers you help in good times watch out.

Do not ask for help if you can help yourself.

New shoes are always uncomfortable.

Do not let the blind be your guide through life.

A person who cannot look you directly in your eyes is dangerous.

The person who wipes his lips with his tongue during a speech is always lying.

The road to happiness is full of thorns.

Live and let live.

Animals do not strike preemptively.

Judas takes money for betrayal.

People in power always manipulate the numbers.

All people are scared of the truth.

Only the most fit should win.

Greedy and lazy people try to carry the most on their shoulders.

Birds sing for pleasure, people sing for money.

The moon and the sun are partners in light, just as husband and wife are partners in life.

People who try to be important use fancy words.

Watch what you do to others. The same treatment will certainly come back to you in your lifetime.

Frogs and men can be cooked alive slowly, often not knowing what is happening to them.

Thieves have long fingers.

Do not ever kill for anybody or you will be next.

A good woman and man are hard to find.

Postponed work and ideas go to waste.

If you do not begin to work on your idea somebody else will.

The older the broom gets, the more he misses.

Keep a journal of your days. You never know when you will need to refer to it.

Always right down your goals. Without them, you drive the roads of your life without a map.

Many people go through the life blindfolded.

A hungry man is dangerous.

A drunken man is stupid.

A crowd creates a false sense of security.

Power lies in the numbers.

It is never they but he.

A man without land is no man.

Many learn how to listen, obey and follow. Few learn how to think, observe and experiment.

The left hand always washes the right hand and vice versa.

In every nation you find bread with two barks. The top is always soft and the bottom is always hard.

If you do not want to get hurt, you never touch high voltage power lines or the government.

Life without family is like a walk through the desert alone.

Nothing is forever. Even stars fall down.

The Devil is the dark side of man.

The God is the good side of man.

Be careful of what you feed your brain.

Never borrow money, pipes and women.

The information that you receive through the eyes is more accurate than the information that you receive through the ears.

Very few people strive for love, family and happiness, but many strive for money.

Your freedom lies bartering.

A soldier's profession is in desperation escaped from one misery to another.

It is very difficult to throw a rock straight up.

Music is a form of divine communication.

Honey always flows freely from a politician's mouth but never from beehives.

If you feel like doing something, hurry, do it, and then sit down.

If you buy cheap, you pay twice.

Work done in a hurry is worthless.

The only truth giver is Mother Nature.

In wine there is truth.

You will never know what nature and a man in power have in store for you.

For gold and truth you must dig very deep.

Guilt is the heaviest thing in life to carry.

You cannot sit on two chairs at the same time.

Never go to the store hungry.

Food always smells best by the bakery door.

You cannot serve two masters.

The sun, wind, water, cold, heat and volcano are the most powerful things in the nature.

Increased value of your dwelling provides you with false feeling that you are rich.

Inflation is a government scam to collect more taxes.

The majority of the people follow beaten path.

Pepper gets man on the shoulders and woman into the grave.

Very few wander off the beaten path.

What is on your tongue is most of the time what is in your heart.

Be aware of a marked man.

A thief will always lie.

Where there is nothing, not even death will go.

The faster you learn, the more mistakes you are allowed to make.

What you obtain easily you will lose easily.

If you are poor, everything around you looks bigger.

It is better to buy clothes for some people than to feed them.

You eat like a horse and drink like a camel.

Things that you buy on credit you cannot afford. It is like raising somebody else's child, as they grow, the ability to pay for them will leave you with nothing.

The one that is smiling last is often smiling the most.

You will never have an idea of what you are actually missing.

Puppets do not have their own words.

Morning has more wisdom then the night before.

If you cannot see it in your mind, it will not happen in your life.

Stay calm and do not argue if you are threatened.

You cannot break the will of man.

For your generosity you will end up in the poor house.

A two-system party is like two lovers.

Greed will make you blind.

The more you get, the more you want.

You are blind and deaf before you reach maturity.

Bees and men are robbed before winter.

Not everything that shines is gold.

True art and music come from the heart, just as truth and beauty.

Look for love and acceptance within yourself and your family first.

Without that love, none other can thrive.

Even a thing can walk to the restroom by itself.

It is difficult to find a drop of reason within a flood of words.

You cannot run away from your problems.

Don't ever put your second born in the driver's seat.

You sort things until you get the worst.

You lose your defenses in time and space.

Insecurity is a tool of destruction.

Many do not see the forest behind the trees.

The more you know the more you remember.

Sometimes the best answer is silence.

Life never tolerates three mistakes.

Men hide in their secrets.

The hand you write with reveals your heart and soul.

You cannot prevent events from occurring.

You cannot make shit without material.

Everybody looks for the easy way out.

You like the colors you see less of.

Everything is beautiful in good times.

When you are down, sing a song. It will help to life your spirits.

If you cannot learn from the two same mistakes you will never learn.

He always chases winds on fields.

He was cutting for so long that he cut his finger off.

Tears are the seeds of future happiness and freedom. Let them rain when they need to fall.

He who seeds the wind will harvest a storm.

What he did not hear, he never spoke about.

A monk has so many books that he has no idea what is in them.

Most of the people use only three senses out of six.

Feed your mind so that your body can grow.

Do not ever worry what people say, they never know for certain.

If you become a radio you cannot receive.

In life, you cannot always win.

Not all books are mothers of knowledge.

Only a child's smile is genuine and true.

Many compete with their own stupidity.

The one who already has is always the one who gets more.

A true melting pot you will find only in America.

Disgrace a woman and you disgrace a nation.

Increase demand by prohibition.

The wealthy make the rules.

A smile is a growing miracle.

You cannot laugh with depressed people.

What you lose in your eyes will get lost in a memory.

Distance and site are the delete keys of the mind.

Time is the best medicine.

Trust in Mother Nature – she will guide you through your life.

Make friends with a tree. It will never let you down and teach you plenty.

If one is in misery he will leave, if many are in misery they will stay.

If you did something good only one will know, but if you did something bad hundreds will know.

A brain saturated with alcohol is always looking for a scapegoat.

Cut your finger before you cut your hand.

Fans keep people in, not out.

Carrying knowledge is easier then carrying your possessions.

Books should never be loaned. They should be given and cherished.

Fertile land always has more weeds.

Every farmer knows that you cannot keep the weeds behind the fence.

Always sweep before your door first.

You cannot wash guilt with water and soap and you cannot drown either.

You cannot get more than you put in.

Do not lose your head. You never know when you will need it.

Nature and animals do not share.

Even a cactus produces a flower once a year.

Speeches of politicians are a half full and half empty.

It is not what you know, but whom you know.

You love somebody only if you think about him more than you think about yourself.

In democracy nobody knows the true leader.

You cannot play if you do not pay.

Where light descends, we will find color.

Nobody can make you rich, only your brain.

Why would somebody a thousand miles away try to make you rich?

One man's misery brings to many happiness.

One man's fortune brings many jealousy.

One man's garbage is for another blessing.

You will never understand why he does not have.

A crocodile without teeth can still bite a man without a brain.

Worker goes for daily bread, businessman for money and politician to screw somebody.

Disappointment of leader is when his speech falls on deaf ears.

Every woman will sometimes uses crocodile tears to get what she wants.

Bananas and troubles always come in bunches.

Manifestation implies that there is an illusion.

The majority of liars and deceivers are always on the top.

A bee will never sting, and a snake will never strike if you do not invade their territory.

Day and night, darkness and blackness have their own territory.

In your life you have two fierce competitors. God wants to save your soul and the government wants your money.

Everybody is holding on his or her skirt sometime in life.

If somebody wishes for you that you would get it, you will.

Buy something for someone, and they will forget from where it came. Make something for someone, and they will always remember.

Don't ever give up your family and your gun.

Call all your dogs.

Everything is possible under the sun.

You must know how to handle love and roses; both of them have thorns.

You scratch my back, I will scratch your back –maybe.

Let us be friends, but I keep mine and you keep yours.

A relationship between a father and son is full of only half-truths.

An independent thinker is dangerous to people in power.

A knowledgeable and possessive man is a good servant.

You can observe more from the top than from the bottom.

It is your choice swim up or down.

You cannot straighten a mature tree.

You can change the lifestyle of a grown up man.

Everybody who works for a living gets kissed in good times and whipped in bad times.

Not everybody who laughs is happy.

Napoleon lost the war because everyone did nothing more than their jobs.

A desperate man surrounds his heart with armor and destroys his brain with alcohol.

Some trees are fruitless, but no tree can give fruit before maturity.

Not all flowers have thorns. Beware of the ones that do – they hide them well.

You can be invited into somebody else's territory, but you will be removed as thorns in the eye if you invade.

Wind fuels the fire.

Not even dogs are divided by color, but they are divided by the jobs they were born to do.

A man who hurts somebody in the heart will apologize, bring flowers, and give a kiss. Only a coward could care less.

An animal will lose its life if handicapped, man loses his life if he loses his pride or his fortune.

The man who lies is also the man who steals.

You will gladly give your life for your offspring. Nothing is as bad as you see it.

True love does not have a price.

Some will bring you happiness and some will bring you misery.

Cowardly people do not care for any one else's well being.

Love cannot be bought on credit.

You will not find milk and honey without work.

Only music has three sides to it. It can bring you happiness, sadness or misery.

Nothing is so far that you cannot reach it.

Your senses are sharpened by fear.

Tobacco and alcohol steals pleasure and time.

Do not burn your bridges, reinforce them.

If you use a gun for the government you become a hero, if you use the gun on your own you become a criminal.

You have to go to the mountain. The mountain will never come to you.

Things that are sold in quantity become cheap and lose value.

Do not feed what you don't want.

Those who are striving to find shortcuts, have no patience.

Even an old bag has a story to tell.

Nothing of value will come easy to you.

Be true to yourself, and you will be true to others.

Take away a man's title and you will find out that he is not any better than you.

Anybody can criticize, but only few can perform.

Man is never satisfied regardless of matter how much he produces.

You can preach only if you are not challenged.

Religion is ritual, and only that.

Love is the only law that should never be broken.

A spineless mans jacket always flies with the wind.

Lies and promises are served on a golden plate accompanied by emotional music to everyone.

Only barbarians and cowards mutilate the body of their enemies.

Thieves are born from opportunity.

Steal a little and they will put you in jail cell. Steal a lot and they will make you a king of the land.

The shoemaker's wife and blacksmith's horse don't have shoes.

Television, if not used properly destroys the family and steals time.

If you abuse your time in front of a television set, you cannot use your brain.

If you say it cannot be done, you admit that you do not know how, everything can be done if you want.

A dog that barks does not bite.

A mother can feed ten children, but ten children are not capable of feeding one mother.

In life you must know from where the wind blows.

If you do not want an enemy, don't give a friend a knife.

Obesity shows disrespect to your body.

Informers get large rewards and a short life.

You must wait for the night before you can judge the day.

To learn patience, watch a spider build his web.

When we believe that all animals are equal, then we can believe that we all are equal.

The sun never shines for one rose.

Give a pig a title and he will show you who he really is.

Nobody ever got rich with honest work.

The truth is always in your hands.

The one who wants everything gets nothing.

Not even a tree can grow to heaven.

Start with gold and you end up with mud.

What the sun shows you during the day, the moon gives to you during the night.

The pride of man is a successful new generation.

Clothes make the man, but will not change the character.

Numbers in a scientist's hand are absolute truth, but in government and politician's hands become absolute lies.

Play their tune and they will follow you to your death.

If you want to go to heaven you must believe in God.

It is hard to get something you want but it is harder to keep it.

Beauty and power are not absolute.

Survival of the nation depends on the reproduction of the fittest and a solid family.

Makeup cannot make you beautiful but virtue will.

Those who do not have money cannot be above the law.
Your immediate family is the pillar of your soul. God is the pillar of your faith. Your family keeps your spirits high. If you lose them your life will become as empty as night in the desert.

Nobody can bring misery upon you – only you can bring it upon yourself.

Out of sight – Out of mind.

Not every story has a happy ending.

You must learn and experience the difficult things in life in order to appreciate the good things.

Don't worry as you go through adolescence. Your life will change every ten years, just as summer and winter bring sunshine or darkness.

Those who believe their own destiny prosper. Those who believe in televised fantasy and propaganda perish.

In the wild kingdom, only the fittest become the leaders. In the human race the opposite is true.

If you are young and in trouble, you call upon your mother. As you get older you call upon God.

Government and the friends you know, you will forget in time. Your mother and God you will never forget.

From the misery that I have brought upon myself from the trust that I put in someone else's hands – you can read all the thoughts and things that I have come up with today.

As the water flows its own way – your offspring will go their way.

Kings handed out titles for free – today you have to pay for them.

People who are successful, more often have a broom in hand than a golden pen.

One out of a million will survive a fall from the sky, but none shall survive if they are rejected by society.

No one can survive life without friends.

Life without your family, life is as lonely as a woman without a partner.

The love of a parent can never be replaced.

Heed the warnings of nature.

The sky is full of stars, but all of them are out of your reach.

Destiny is a path we all walk alone.

The ocean is full of fish, but only a few provide your body with nutrition.

Art and beauty are in the eye of the beholder.

Not all water is drinkable.

Be careful what you feed your body with.

Learn how to read between the lines.

After your third glass, you will lose your tongue.

After the fourth glass, the truth will come out.

Behind every successful son is a father.

It is easy to manipulate and downgrade people if you have the upper hand.

Do not ever think that because you have a title, you are better than the next person.

A title is only a label given to you. It means nothing of who you are.

Without goals, a man is lost.

Without dreams, a man is empty.

Without family, a man is alone.

In life, sometimes you will be up, and other times you will be down.

Behave accordingly.

Be aware of the power you have over other people.

Lies blossom as weeds to hide a simple flower of truth.

Think twice before you speak. Sometime you may be on the receiving end of the words you speak.

Night always follows the day, just the sun always rises after the night ends.

If you abuse your power, in time you too will be abused.

All people have a good and an evil side to them. Be aware of which is stronger within you.

If you have a difficult life in your youth, your old age will be smooth and easy.

Even the strongest power lines can burn out over time.

If you don't respect towards others, others will not respect you.

You cannot like some one else if you don't care about yourself.

Arrogance breeds enemies.

A diploma will not guarantee your place in life.

Your persistence and your personality are your greatest strengths.

What you know is the equivalent of a golden bottom. WHO you know is equivalent to a reinforced steel bottom.

Knowledge and self-respect are the two things that no one can take away from you.

Rudeness projects misery and self-loathing.

Be good to the devil and he will reward you with hell.

What you cannot find in the brain, you can make up for with muscle.

Favors and unfulfilled promises will destroy a friendship.

Only health, happiness, and family are priceless.

Many people try to find happiness in a bottle. Others still look for happiness in gambling.

Every piece of land is different, just as every man is different.

Nature provides us with life, and in return we give her garbage and disrespect.

For an honest man, his word is a binding contract. For a dishonest man, his word is a tool used to manipulate others.

The only position in life that is everlasting is the one you create for yourself.

What has been given to you can always be just as easily taken away from you.

You are free only in your dreams.

Beware of the rules you apply to others. One day you will have to follow them yourself.

Don't ever say to another, "Do you know who I am?"

Naked you came into this world, and naked you shall depart.

Our policies have changed from the carrot and a stick to lies and daisy bombs.

The man who cannot organize his own house will try to organize the houses of others.

Only a secured government can spy on its own people.

You will not find wisdom in all elder people; however, children always speak the truth.

If you have a good product, you do not need a brash salesman.

You cannot fool a fox twice.

If you close your eyes, it does not mean that you are sleeping.

Give wisdom, keep your memories.

Nothing in life can bring more sadness than the man who does not appreciate the sacrifices that have been made for him.

If you want to lose a friend, loan them money.

What you don't want to have, lend it to someone.

Travel to your homeland at least once in your life. Your history is in your roots.

Don't spit in the well. You never know when you will have to drink the water from it.

The ones who have nothing want everything.

Man can reason with anyone but a greedy man.

It takes an entire lifetime to build a reputation. It takes a mere moment to destroy it.

The one who loves only gold, loves nothing, not even himself.

Only God and farmers truly know what people need.

Learn from your family.

Your family will always be the most honest with you.

The man who is not happy with what he has, does not deserve to have more.

Don't offer your opinion if you are not asked to speak.

Too much shelter can damage what could have been a strong tree.

You must think ten times before you speak.

Always check your information to ensure that it is accurate before you offer it as advice.

Einstein had a short memory – but he knew where to look to find the answers.

Your voice on the telephone reveals much about you to the person on the other end of the line.

Never say "no" to a customer. No is a word for children.

People do not want to hear your stories. They want you to listen to theirs.

Stop being a radio and become a receiver. You will learn more throughout your life this way.

Live your life to the fullest each day. You never know when it will end.
Memories made together are the most cherished gifts.

A photograph can capture the soul of a moment in time.

Hold onto your dreams, they are the only thing you have that is truly your own.

Find solace in a good book.

Printed in the United States
23541LVS00001B/694-744